ColoringBook

By Banana leaves

.................................................................

Colorist's Name

.................................................................

Date

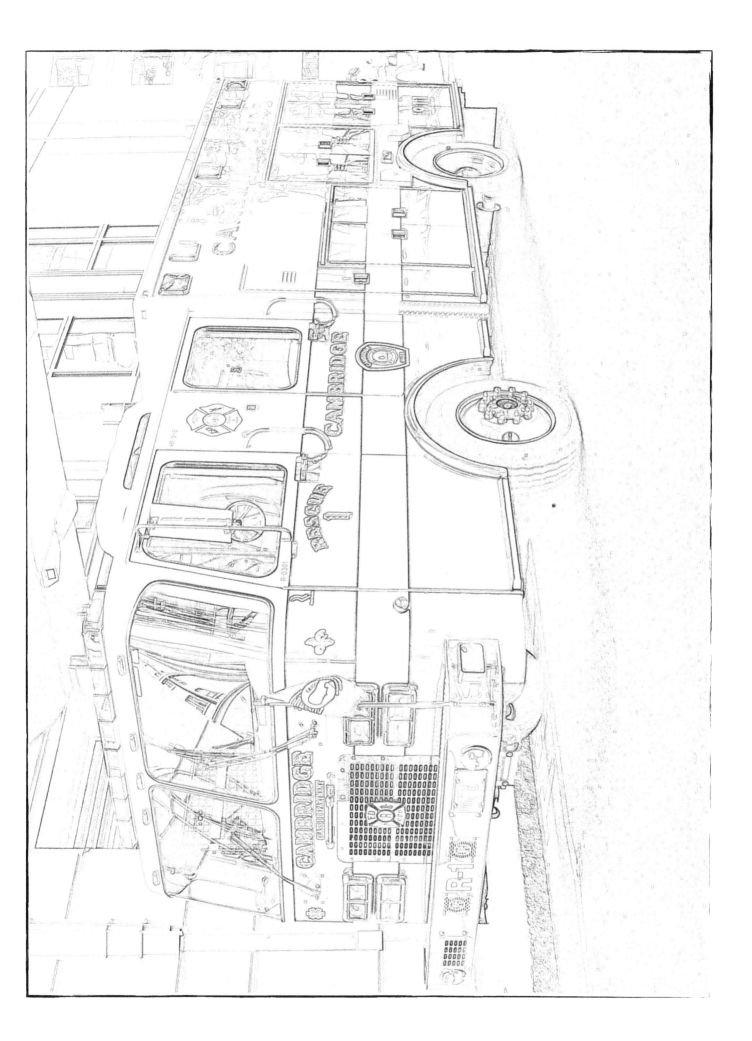

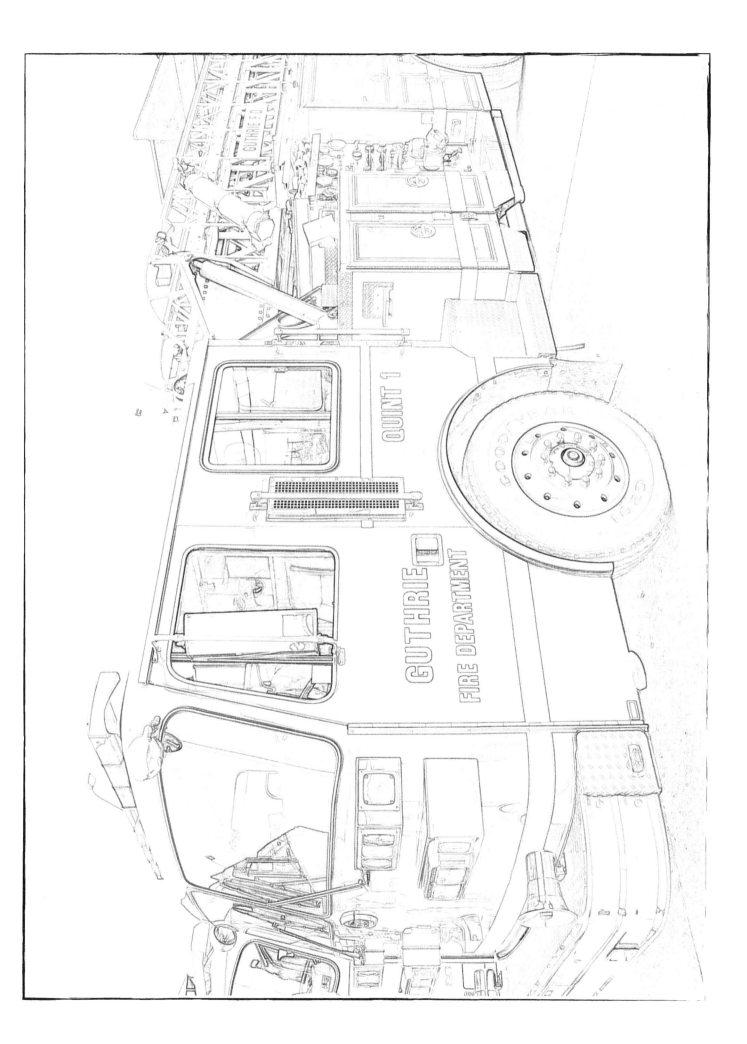

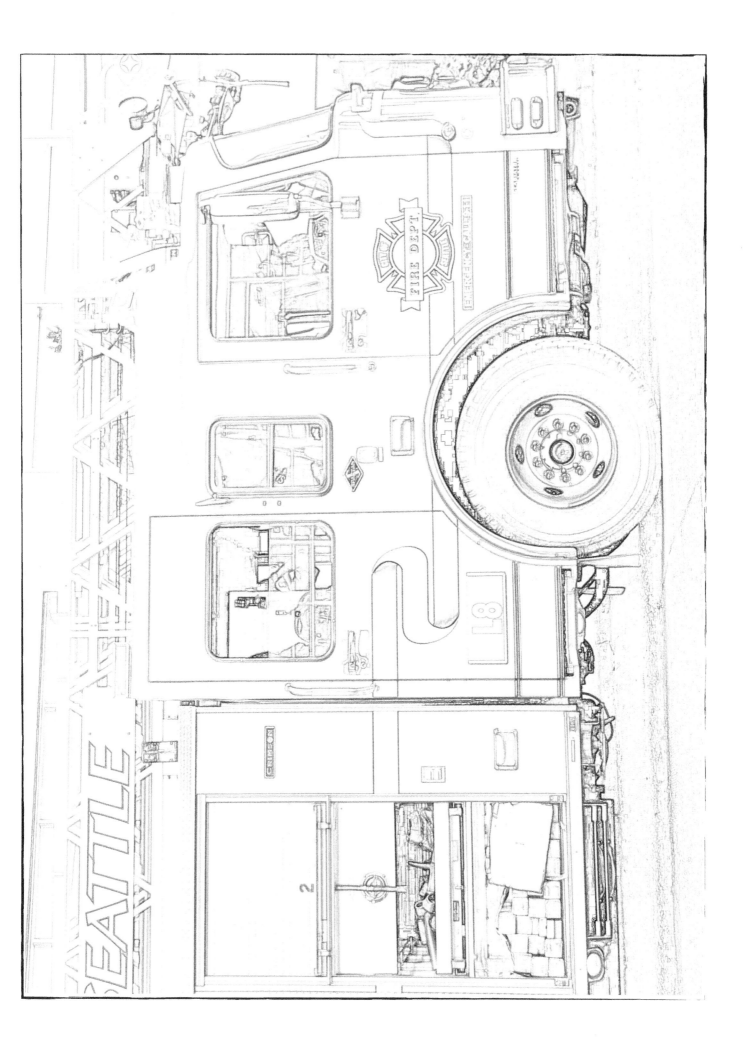

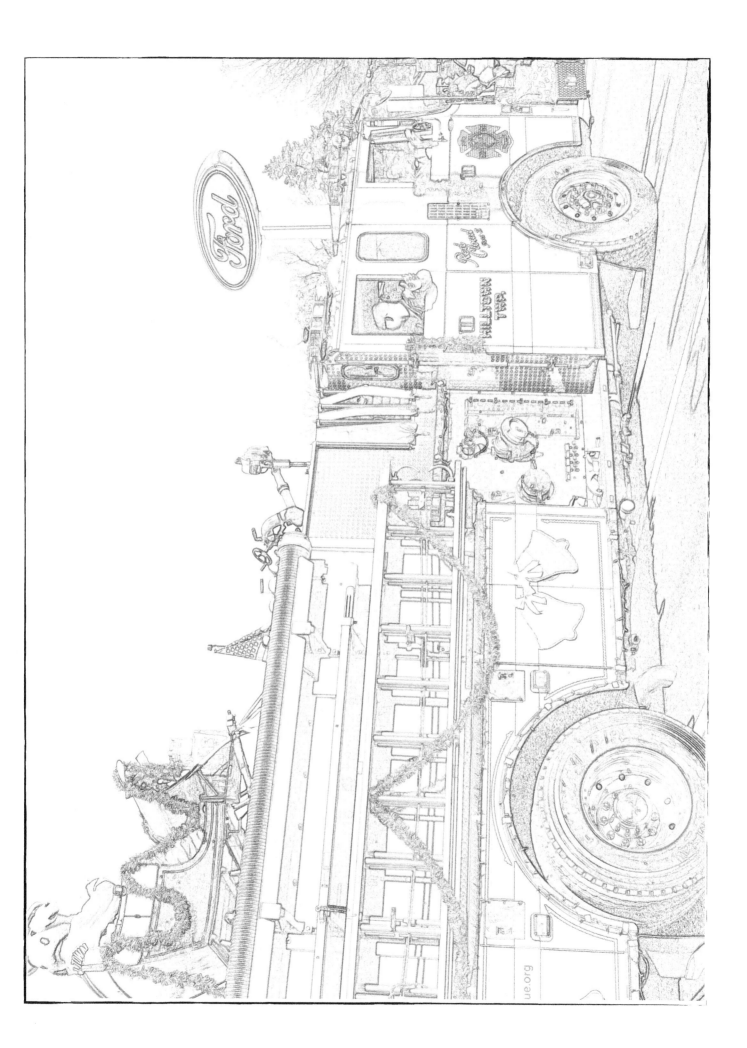

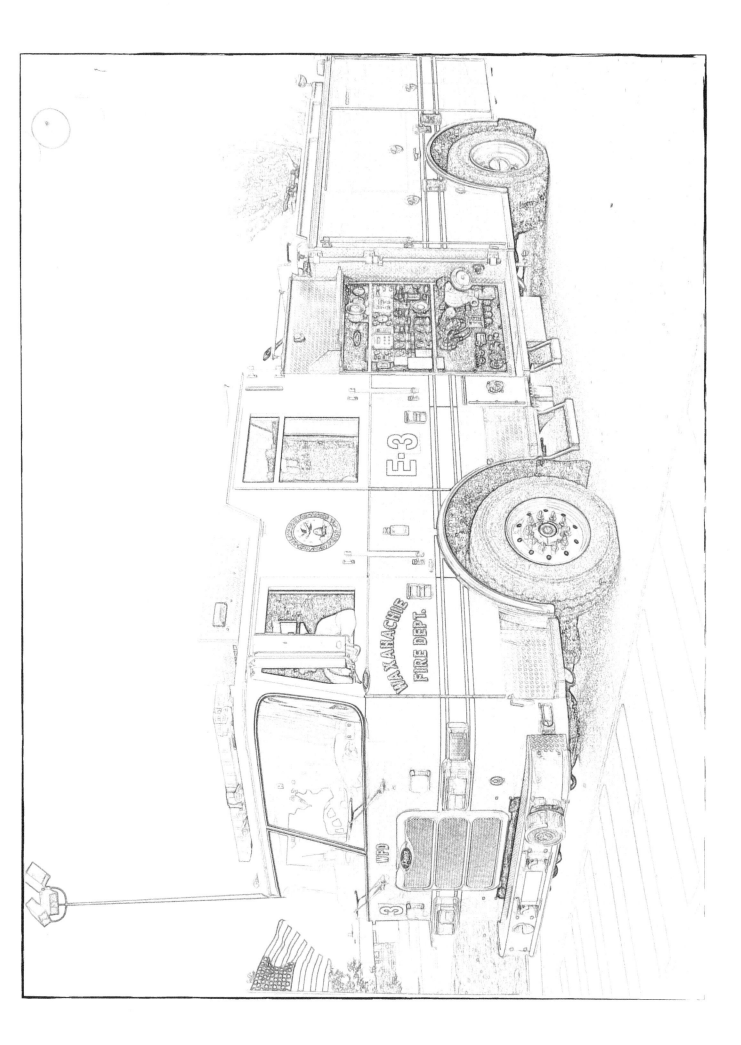

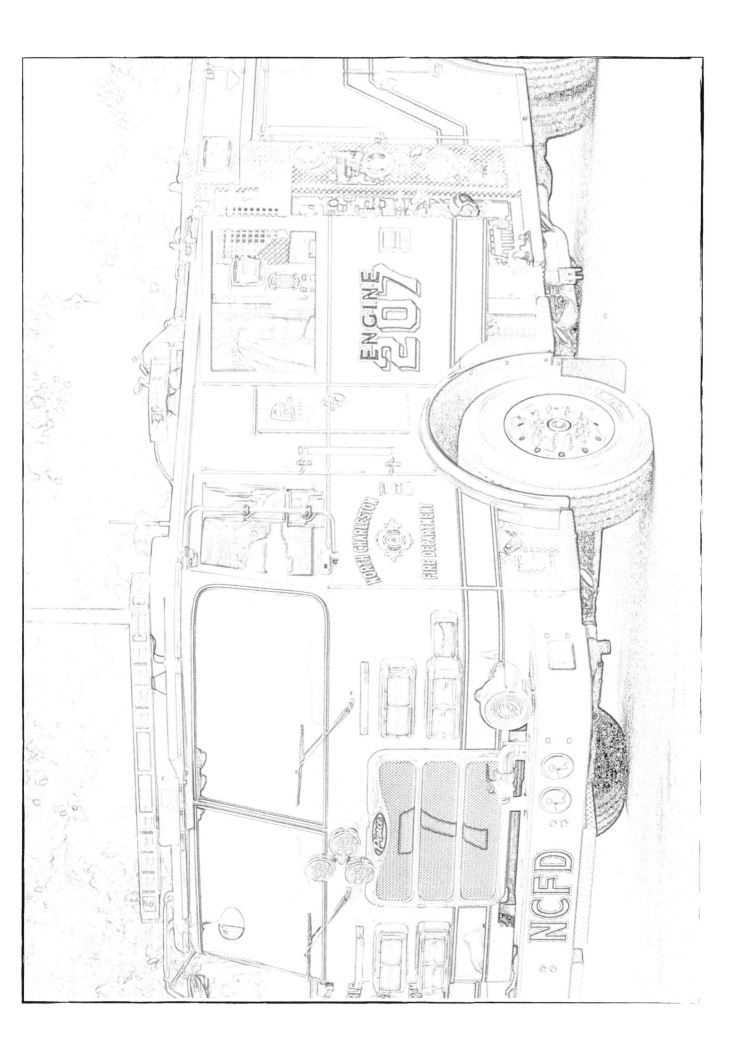

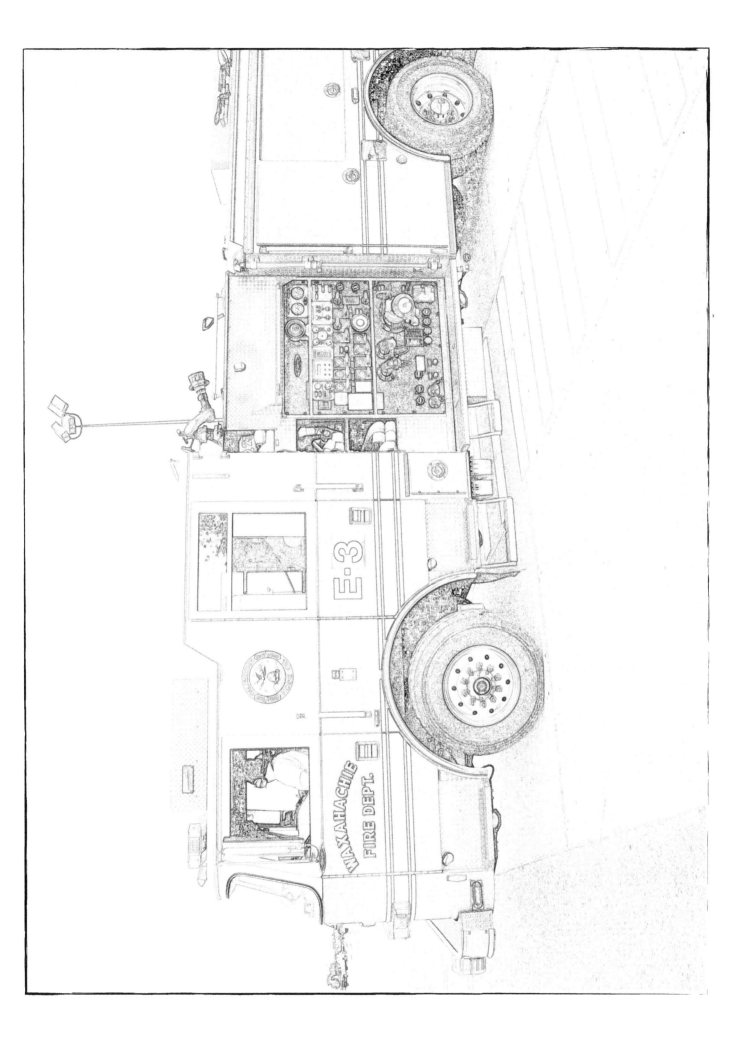

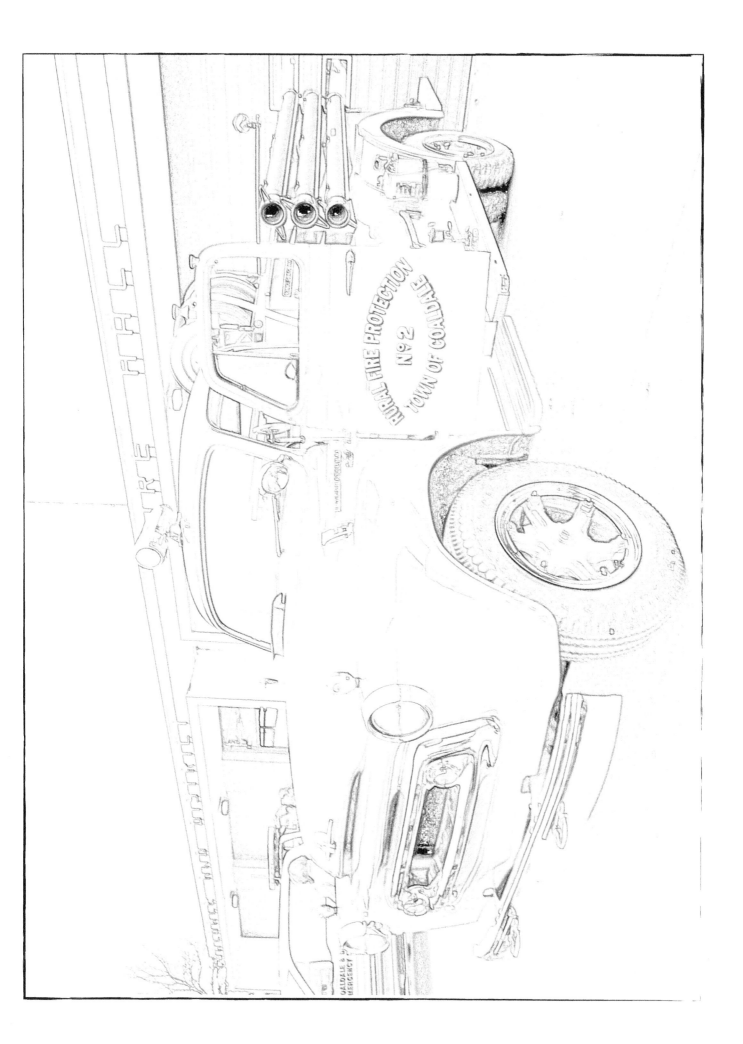

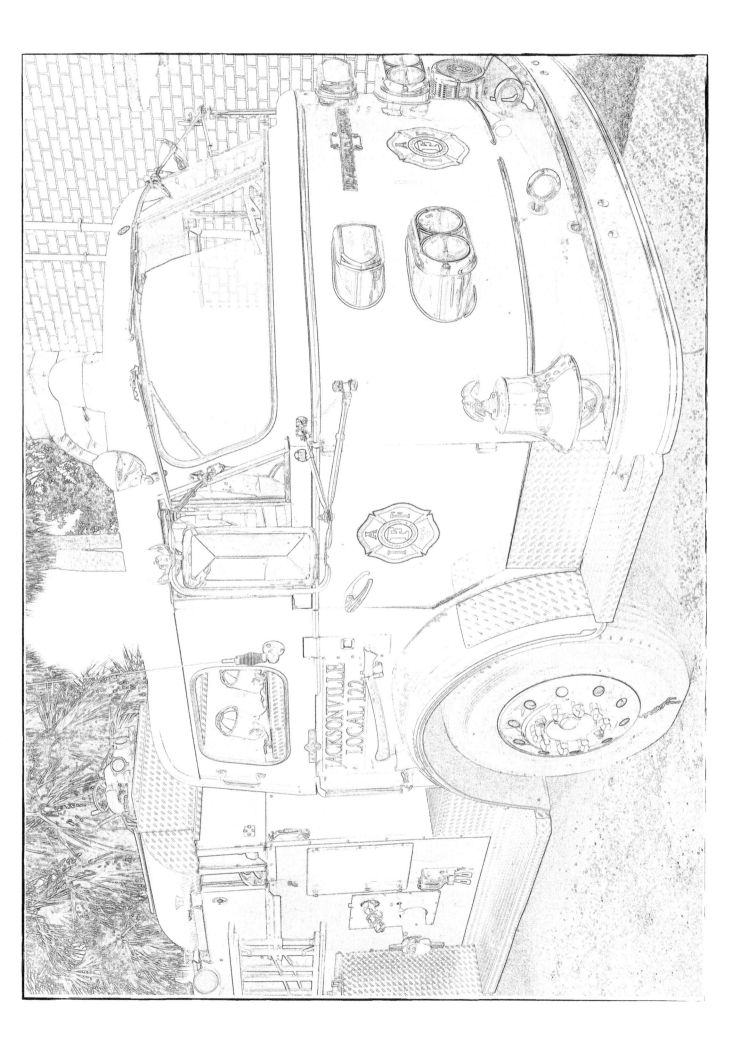

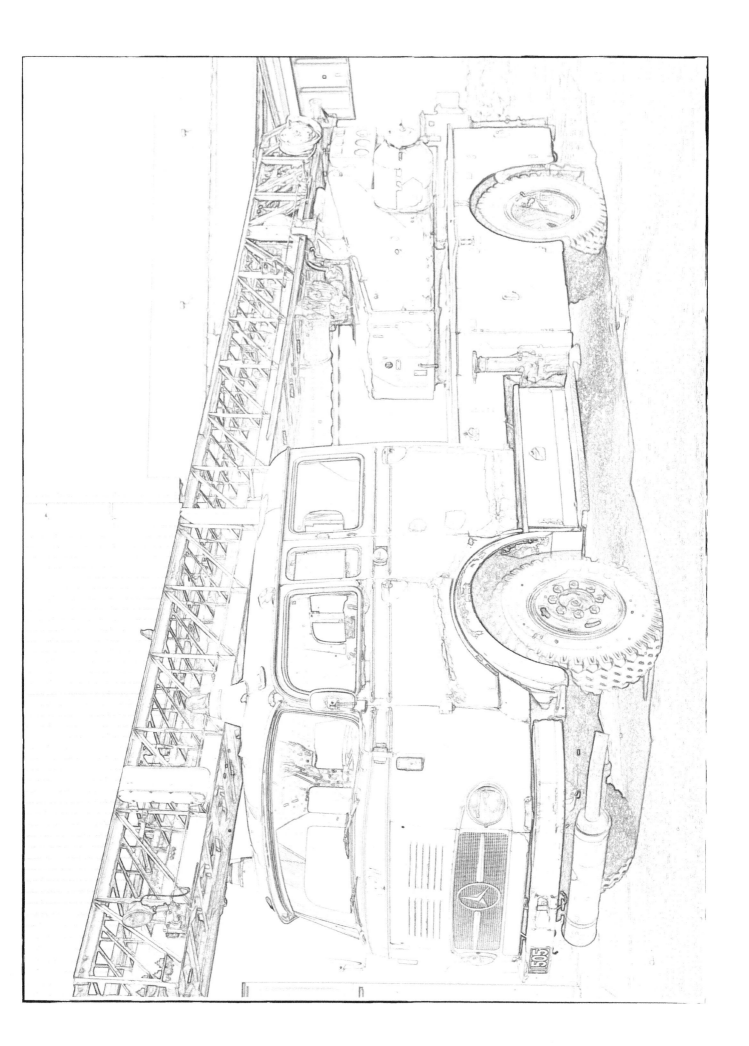

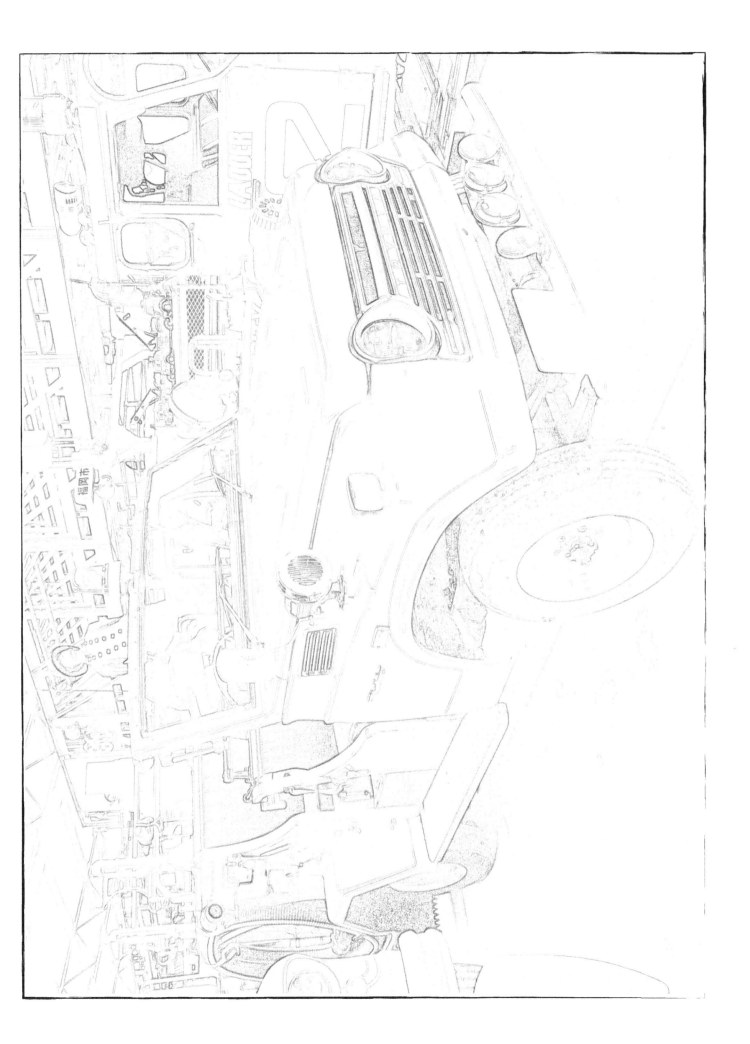

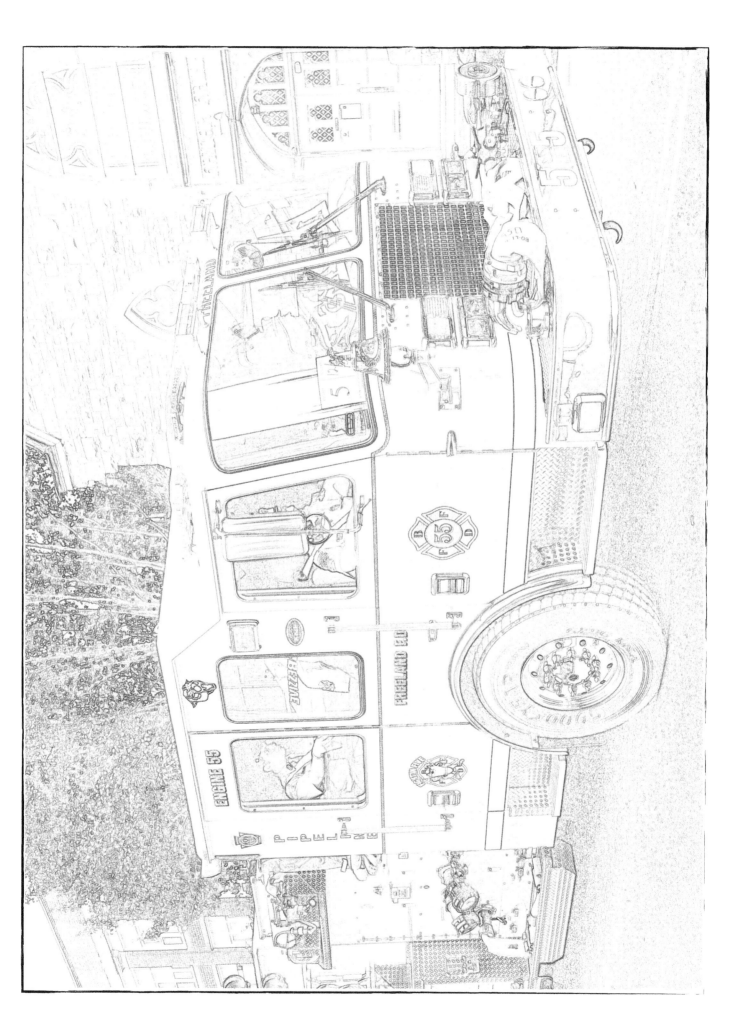

Made in the USA
Coppell, TX
27 May 2023

17371600R00037